BACKYARD BIOMES

THERE'S A FOREST IN MY BACKYARD!

By Walter LaPlante

Gareth Stevens
PUBLISHING

Please visit our website, www.garethstevens.com. For a free color catalog of all our high-quality books, call toll free 1-800-542-2595 or fax 1-877-542-2596.

Library of Congress Cataloging-in-Publication Data

Names: LaPlante, Walter, author.
Title: There's a forest in my backyard! / Walter LaPlante.
Other titles: There is a forest in my backyard
Description: New York : Gareth Stevens Publishing, [2017] | Series: Backyard
  biomes | Includes bibliographical references and index.
Identifiers: LCCN 2016027228| ISBN 9781482455595 (pbk. book) | ISBN
  9781482455601 (6 pack) | ISBN 9781482455618 (library bound book)
Subjects: LCSH: Forest ecology–Juvenile literature. | Forests and
  forestry–Juvenile literature.
Classification: LCC QH541.5.F6 L3657 2017 | DDC 577.3–dc23
LC record available at https://lccn.loc.gov/2016027228

Published in 2017 by
Gareth Stevens Publishing
111 East 14th Street, Suite 349
New York, NY 10003

Designer: Andrea Davison-Bartolotta and Bethany Perl
Editor: Kristen Nelson

Photo credits: p. 1 Olga Danylenko/Shutterstock.com; pp. 2–24 (background texture) wongwean/Shutterstock.com; p. 5 Anna Nahabed/Shutterstock.com; p. 7 (world map) ekler/Shutterstock.com; p. 7 (forest) amadeustx/Shutterstock.com; p. 9 Skylines/Shutterstock.com; p. 11 (forest) metriognome/Shutterstock.com; p. 11 (pine needles) Beata Becla/Shutterstock.com; p. 11 (beech leaf) Oprea George/Shutterstock.com; p. 13 (beech leaves) SJ Travel Photo and Video/Shutterstock.com; p. 13 (oak leaves) Snowboy/Shutterstock.com; p. 13 (maple leaves) Dmitrij Skorobogatov/Shutterstock.com; p. 15 Ivakoleva/Shutterstock.com; p. 17 Ronnie Howard/Shutterstock.com; p. 19 worldswildlifewonders/Shutterstock.com; p. 21 aldorado/Shutterstock.com.

Printed in the United States of America

CPSIA compliance information: Batch #CW17GS: For further information contact Gareth Stevens, New York, New York at 1-800-542-2595.

CONTENTS

Boldface words appear in the glossary.

Do You See Trees?

Look around you. Are there a lot of trees growing near your house? You might have a forest in your backyard! A forest is a **biome** made up of mostly trees.

Find Forests

Forests grow in places that have some warmer months and get a lot of rain each year. Most **temperate** forests are found in North America, eastern Asia, and western Europe. Some can be found in South America and Australia.

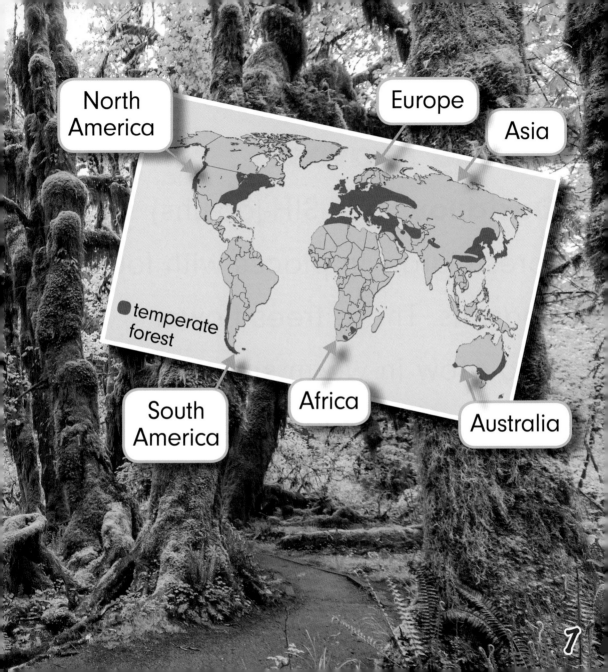

North America

Europe

Asia

● temperate forest

South America

Africa

Australia

Falling Leaves

Deciduous (dih-SIH-joo-uhs) forests grow in places with four seasons. These trees flower and grow in warm springs and summers. They lose their leaves as it gets colder in the fall. Then, they don't grow during cold winters.

summer

fall

winter

spring

9

Always Green

Evergreen forests often grow where summers are warm, but winters aren't very cold. They need a lot of rain. Evergreen forests are made up of needleleaf trees, broadleaf trees, or both. These trees keep their leaves all year round.

needleleaves

broadleaf

Common Trees

Whether your backyard is in North America or Asia, you might see trees from the same family! Temperate forests can be a mix of deciduous and evergreen trees. Beech, oak, and maple trees are commonly found in temperate forests.

13

The Canopy

The top **layer** of the forest is called the canopy. It's made of the leaves of the tallest trees. They sometimes grow so close together they may block the sun! This can keep many plants from growing on the ground. Those that do are often small.

Biome Home

Forests give many animals a home. Some, like birds, even live *in* the trees! They eat the many bugs that live in forests. Other animals, such as foxes, eat small animals like chipmunks that also live in the forest.

cardinal

Animals in a forest biome need to **adapt** to the many seasons. Many birds **migrate** to places where there's more food in winter. Bears and other animals hibernate, or sleep, through the coldest months.

19

Temperate forests are a popular home for another animal—people! However, some people cut trees down to build roads and houses. A forest becomes a backyard without any thought to what's living there. We need to care for this biome!

GLOSSARY

adapt: to change to suit conditions

biome: a natural community of plants and animals, such as a forest or desert

deciduous: falling off after a time of growth

evergreen: staying green

layer: one part of something found over another

migrate: to move to warmer or colder places for a season

temperate: mild weather that's not too hot or too cold

FOR MORE INFORMATION

BOOKS

Silverman, Buffy. *Let's Visit the Evergreen Forest*. Minneapolis, MN: Lerner Publications, 2016.

Waxman, Laura Hamilton. *Life in a Forest*. Minneapolis, MN: Bellwether Media, 2016.

WEBSITES

Biomes
online.kidsdiscover.com/unit/biomes
Find out more about the many biomes of Earth.

Temperate Forest
kids.nceas.ucsb.edu/biomes/temperateforest.html
Read more about deciduous forests here.

INDEX